Turning Back the Pages
Old Broad Marsh & Narrou

Preface

This is the latest title in the Libraries, Archives and Information Publications Group *Turning Back the Pages* series. It is also the first of these popular photographic publications to feature part of the city of Nottingham and the first to be compiled by the staff of Nottinghamshire Archives. It has been produced by Chris Weir, Senior Archivist (Public Services) and Nick Smith, Archives Assistant, largely from photographs and documents held by Nottinghamshire Archives, including images taken from the Nottingham & District Co-operative collection (DD GN) and the City Design & Property Services negatives (CA DP). This publication presents an unrivalled view of the development of Broad Marsh and Narrow Marsh over the last one hundred years.

Mark Dorrington, Principal Archivist

View of Red Lion Street, Narrow Marsh including The Loggerheads public house, during the area's demolition in 1934. The pub remained standing after most of the area was demolished.

Front Cover: Lewis Square, Broad Marsh in the early 1930s. The enclosed courtyard of back-to-back houses had just a single water tap in the yard.

Introduction

In mediaeval times the south side of Nottingham, from the original Saxon borough, on its imposing sandstone cliff, down to the River Leen would have been an inhospitable marshy area. Though development would have been difficult on this poorly drained land there is documentary evidence that there was some settlement in the area. In particular the Marshes provided a home for the Grey Friars and the 'order' gave its name to Grey Friar Gate.

Mediaeval Deed.
This deed was for two tenements of John de Hertil, a tanner, in Broad Marsh (magno marisco) that stood opposite the wall of the Friar's Minor (Grey Friars), 1339.
Nottinghamshire Archives CA 4379

As Nottingham expanded and housing was needed for industrial workers, especially in textiles, the Marshes soon became covered with a dense network of streets. By the early 20th century Broad Marsh and Narrow Marsh had become a highly populated area of overcrowded yards and alleyways. Many of the houses were defective back-to-back dwellings. Its crowded streets were built on marshy, low-lying, land that ran down to the Nottingham Canal and the area suffered from every kind of fever and disease. Yet photographs of that time reveal a flourishing community, with busy shops and services. A 1922 list of occupations for the area underlines the diverse working lives of local people. It includes lace hands, hosiery workers, charwomen, labourers, shopkeepers, navvies, miners, carters, hawkers, street musicians, pedlars and even a 'showman'. Oral history memories of that time suggest that while life could be difficult there was much pride in the local community. One former resident remembers that sanitary conditions were 'terrible....the toilet used to be across the yard and the tap was shared with the men's lodging house. There was no water, no gas, nowhere where you could wash you or anything'. Yet at the same time this resident recalls that though 'the Marsh was the roughest of the rough, the people had good hearts. You never seen anybody want'.

The Corporation's attempts to improve housing and health conditions led to major redevelopment in the 1920s. Following demolition of the Red Lion Street area a Council estate was constructed and further major change came in the early 70s when work began on building the Broad Marsh Shopping Centre. To make way for the Centre it proved necessary to demolish Drury Hill, one of Nottingham most historic streets. The original street pattern, especially of Broad Marsh, and existing communities would never be the same again as a new Nottingham emerged in the 1970s. The Broad Marsh Centre opened in 1975, providing new shopping facilities for the city, complete with a large new car park and bus station. Nottingham was changing rapidly. Today Broad Marsh and Narrow Marsh stand on then threshold of yet another era of change following a grant of outline planning permission for an entirely new Broad Marsh Centre.

This publication highlights the development of one of Nottingham's most fascinating inner-city areas, yet one that rarely features in standard histories of Nottingham. The images used concentrate principally on the 20th century, a key period in the history of Broad Marsh and Narrow Marsh. It is hoped they will evoke feeling and memories of living in the Marsh or just walking through its maze of old streets.

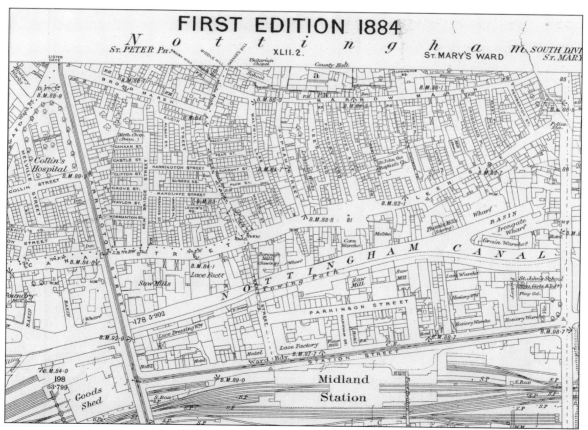

Ordnance Survey Map showing Broad and Narrow Marsh, 1884. It highlights a maze of streets and courtyards.

Marsh Farm House.

This house once stood in Byron Yard, Narrow Marsh, a survival of an earlier age. It was a part-timbered building that would originally have had a thatched roof. At some time it was converted for use as a shop.

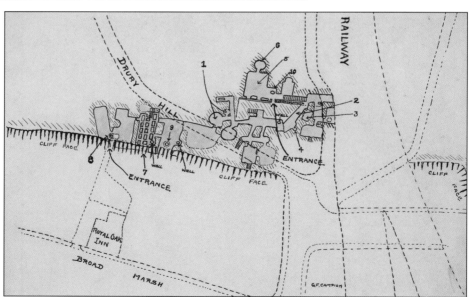

Plan of Caves. This plan of caves under part of Drury Hill was undertaken in the 1930s during the course of archaeological excavations. Some of these caves were adapted as air raid shelters during World War Two.
Nottinghamshire Archives M 1483/1

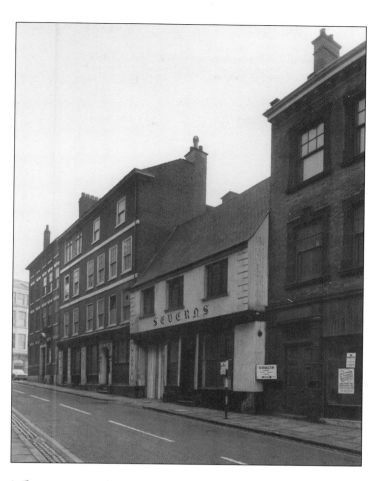

The Severn's Building in 1968.

Severn's is shown here in its original 'home' on Middle Pavement in 1968. It was a wine merchants for many years.

The Severn's Building in 1970. Severn's was a fine mediaeval timbered structure that was moved from Middle Pavement to Castle Road in order

to make way for the new Broad Marsh Centre. At that time it was painstakingly restored.

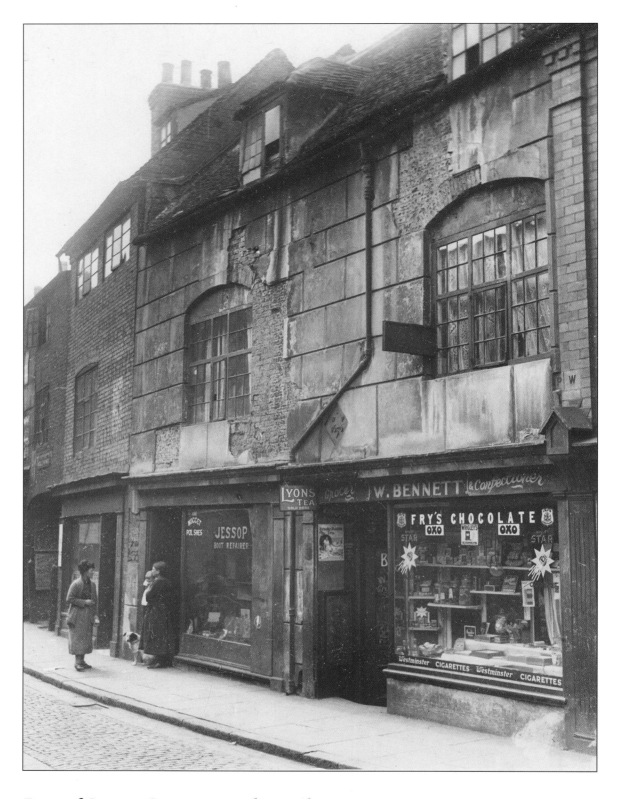

Part of Sussex Street, Broad Marsh. Though the photograph was taken in 1928 it is thought that the shop buildings date from the mid-seventeenth century.

Collin's Hospital. These almshouses stood on Carrington Street. The illustration is from Orange's 'History of Nottingham', 1840. Abel Collins was a wealthy merchant of Nottingham who left substantial funds in his will of 1704 for charitable purposes. Some of these funds were used by trustees to establish several almshouses in the town.

Sherwood Place, Broad Marsh, 1934. The enclosed courtyard received little sunlight and was badly ventilated, contributing to the inhabitants' poor health.

Lodging House.

The Lodgings were on Red Lion Street, Narrow Marsh, 1933. There was a concentration of lodging houses in the area. This reflects the migrant nature of the working population and that many people in the area could not afford their own properties.

Back-to-back Houses. Poor housing conditions are evident in this photograph of Grove Street, Broad Marsh c 1933. The upper storeys were lace dressing rooms. Drainage was along open gutters and water was only available from communal taps in the yards.

December 1922.

R E D   L I O N   S T R E E T   A R E A.

SUMMARY OF OCCUPATIONS.
FEMALES.

Occupation	No.	Occupation	No.
Houseworkers	188	Stall Holders	2
Charwomen	42	Bacon Washer	1
Lace (Dressing Room) Hands	29	Blind Scalloper	1
Hawkers	26	Boarding House Keeper	1
Shopkeepers	20	Blind Pensioner	1
Lace (Home)	16	Beggar	1
Old Age Pensioners	14	Cook	1
Cotton Winders	9	Cotton Doubler	1
Invalids	9	Frame Clipper	1
Hosiery Hands	7	Fish Frier	1
Lace Hands	7	French Polisher	1
Machinists	6	Hosiery Winder	1
Boxmakers	4	Knitter (Jumpers)	1
Pedlars	3	Lace (Clipping)	1
Cotton Preparers	2	Lace Mender	1
Cotton Cleaners	2	No legitimate occupation	1
Charity Lodging House Keepers	2	Overlooker (Dressing Room)	1
Domestic Servants	2	Parish Relief	1
Errand Girls	2	Pensioner (Army)	1
Hair Net Finishers	2	Packer	1
Lodging House Keepers	2	Printer	1
Lace Jenniers	2	Pattern Girl	
Lace Curtain Hands	2	Tailoress	
Net Menders	2	Waitress	
Net Doublers	2	Waste Sorter	
Rag Gatherers	2	Window Cleaner	

December 1922.

R E D   L I O N   S T R E E T   A R E A.

SUMMARY OF OCCUPATIONS.
MALES.

Occupation	No.	Occupation	No.
Labourers	201	Errand Boys	3
Hawkers	80	Ice Cream Vendors	3
Army Pensioners	31	Street Musicians	3
Miners	23	Electricians	2
Old Age Pensioners	22	Fish Friers	2
Newsvendors	16	Gardeners	2
Carters	14	Hosiery Hands	2
Navvies	13	Mat Menders	2
Outporters	11	News Agents	2
Shopkeepers	11	Porters (Coal)	2
Lace Bleachers	7	Printers	2
Coal Dealers	6	Printer's Apprentices	2
Lace Dressers	6	Ship Winders	2
Moulders	6	Tailors	2
Porters	6	Upholsterers	2
Parish Relief	6	Brass Bobbin Winder	1
Window Cleaners	6	Brass Bobbin Maker	1
Fitters	5	Builder	1
Brickmakers	4	Boiler Maker	1
Beggars	4	Blacksmith's Striker	1
Glass and China Rivetters	4	Bagsman	1
General Dealers	4	Butcher's Assistant	1
Invalids	4	Bill Distributor	1
Lace Makers	4	Boxmaker	1
Pedlars	4	Bookbinder	1
Stall Holders	4	Billiard Marker	1
Umbrella Repairers	4	Boot Repairer	1
Bricklayers	3	Cooper	1

Lists of Occupations.

The 'occupation' lists for 'Males' and 'Females' were compiled by the Corporation in 1922. They highlights the wide range of occupations in the area. Many women were employed in housework, with no less than 42 given as 'charwomen'. Many women were also employed in the lace and hosiery trade. Of the men, 201 were recorded as 'labourers', 80 were 'hawkers' and 31 were 'army pensioners'.

Nottinghamshire Archives
CA TC 18/121/6/3

LACE CURTAINS from 1/- per pair.   LACES, EDGING, PINAFORES AND APRONS.
Splendid Assortment.   Exceptional Prices.
                                    LACE MANUFACTURER.
W. COTTON,   Weekday Cross,
Established over 50 Years.   NOTTINGHAM.

Advertisement 1908

from Wright's commercial directory for the lace curtains of W. Cotton of Weekday Cross, 1908. At that time lace goods from Nottingham were being exported all over the world.

Advertisement for Player's.

The advert was for Player's Castle tobacco factory, Broad Marsh and Beast Market Hill. This is where John Player, founder of the giant tobacco company, first started his business in Nottingham. Brands like Player's 'Navy Cut' soon became household words throughout the country.

TOBACCO DEALERS.

READY MONEY *versus* CREDIT.

Buy your Tobacco of the Manufacturer and save a Profit.

Special advantages to Cash Buyers.

PLAYER'S

CASTLE TOBACCO FACTORY,

BROAD MARSH,

AND

BEAST MARKET HILL,

NOTTINGHAM.

Good Tobacco from 3s. 3d. per lb., and upwards.

Price Lists on application.

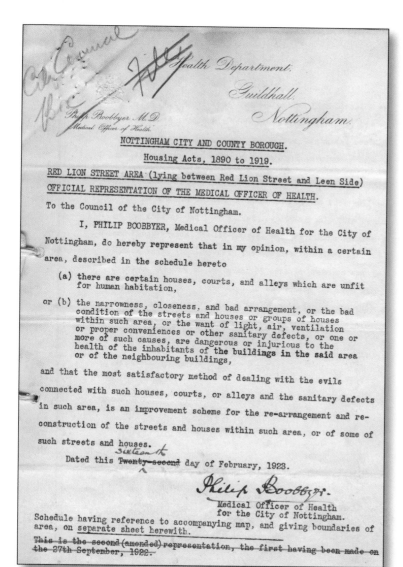

Red Lion Street in the 1920s.

In the early 1920s the Red Lion Street area was declared 'unfit for human habitation'. An inspection by the Medical Officer of Health had revealed a large number of 'sanitary defects'. Following the report an 'improvement area' was scheduled and many streets and houses were demolished.

Nottinghamshire Archives CA TC 10/121/6/12

Oral History Transcript

This edited extract was from an interview with a resident of Red Lion Street. (Courtesy of Nottingham City Council , Leisure & Community Services, Nottingham Central Library).

What was the house like? Oh terrible. One down and one up. No water, no gas, nowhere you could wash or anything. The toilet used to be across the yard and the tap was in the yard – there was us and there used to be a lodging house next door.

What games did you used to play when you were growing up?
Only knocking on doors and running off. We always used to be sitting on the roads under the Loggerheads and singing.

Red Lion Street. The street was originally known as 'Narrow Marsh'. The photograph shows the entrance to Foundry Yard in 1930.

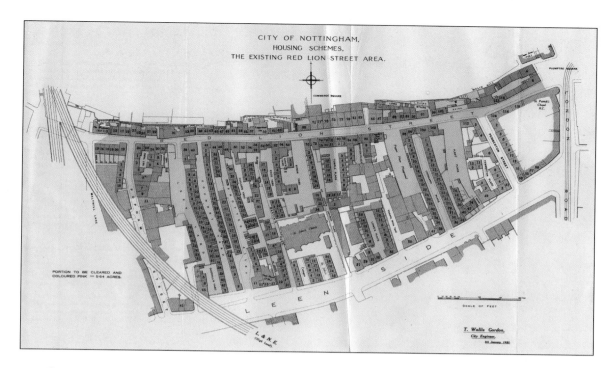

Red Lion Street 1923. The existing 'Red Lion Street Area', as delineated in a plan of 1923. The plan was included in a Corporation report on the area's redevelopment.

Nottinghamshire Archives CA TC 10/121/6/12

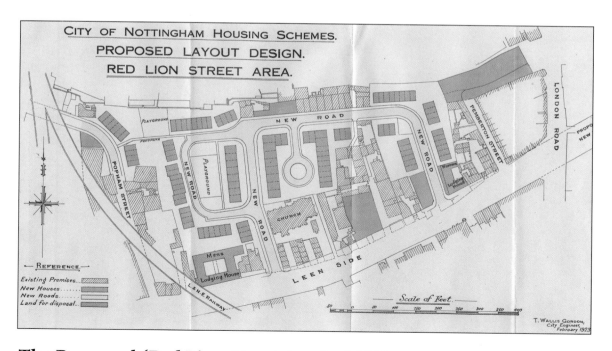

The Proposed 'Red Lion Street Area' of 1923. A development of Council houses eventually replaced most of the original houses.

Narrow Marsh 1934.

The photograph shows the area after most of the buildings had been knocked down. The spire of St. John's Church can be seen at the right hand end of the view. The church was destroyed by enemy bomb damage during the war.

Part of Cliff Road (formerly Red Lion Street) in 2006. Some Council houses are at the front of the photograph and St. Mary's Church tower is at the back of the view.

Police Photographs. Both photographs were taken in the early 1900s, one of Allen Leonardi and the other of Elizabeth Mart. They both lived at an 'LH' (Lodging House) in Narrow Marsh. Elizabeth had a number of tattoos, including 'two hearts' and 'Love'. It was noted that Allen Leonardi, alias William Brown, alias Herbert Smith, was fingerprinted on 18 July 1908.

Nottinghamshire Archives CA PO 4/18/8

Canaan (Methodist) Street Church. The Church was the centre of a Sisterhood that attempted to improve local living conditions. The building suffered bomb attacks in both world wars. It was closed in 1948.

Nottinghamshire Archives NC MR 15/28

Canaan Church Social League Sisterhood, 1910. The 'Marsh Sisterhood' was formed in November 1909, with the financial help of Jesse Boot, the founder of Boots The Chemists.

Objects of the Marsh Sisterhood

Canaan Street Church 'Sports Fayre' 1937.

The Marsh Sisterhood arranged all kinds of activities, ranging from church functions to sports events.

Nottinghamshire Archives
NC MR 15/72

Extract from Kelly's *Directory* for 1912.

The entries provide an insight into different trades and occupations of people who lived and worked in the area. It includes 'principal occupants' for Valentine Place but such a list was not in any way comprehensive and many ordinary people living on the street would not be recorded.

BROAD MARSH.
(Lister gate.) My.

1½ Crampton & Son, plumbers
3 Senior Rd. drpr. & Mchstr. whsmn
5-7 Henton W. H. & Co. Limited, grocers' outfitters
9-11 Dunnicliffe George H. v. Black's Head
15-17 Fleeman Robert & Sons Ltd. smallware dealers
.... Chancery place ....
19 Solari Mrs. Ellen, hard confectnr
25 Sansam Miss Mary Ann, news agt
27 Issott George, fishmonger & fruitr
.... Valentine place ....
29 Gray Edwin, milk dealer
31 Lakin Thomas, herb beer maker
33 Collinson Samuel, painter
35 Inkin Mrs. M. A. wardrobe dealer
37 Blank William, pork butcher
.... Sherwood place ....
39 Holland Albert, v. Old Royal Oak
41 Singleton Bonser, boot maker
43 Lomas George, printer
43a, Horsburgh Jn. Chas. lithographer
45 Burch Robert, paper merchant
47 Linsky L. & Co. cabinet makers
51 & 53 Ward George, hair dresser & tobacconist
Middle marsh...Sussex st...(Cross over
36 Turner C. H. & Co. blouse manfrs
30, 32 & 34 Rowntree Ltd. chocolate manufacturers
24 Fleeman Robert & Sons Limited, smallware dealers
.... New Bridge street ....
Primitive Methodist Chapel
16a, Dexter George, saddler
16 Gray E. & Son, butchers
Harrington Bros. Nottingham Ltd. wholesale drapers
St. Peter's Parish Room
10 Hooley Mrs. Sarah, beer retailer & shopkeeper
.... Berwick place ....
Harrington Bros. Nottingham Ltd. drapers
4 Atkinson Robert, fent dealer
2 Solari Mrs. Ellen, hard confectnr

Crimean and Indian Mutiny Veterans' Association.

DEAR SIR,

We regret to have to inform you that on Sunday last, W. Carlisle, late of the 7th Foot, died at his residence, 1, Valentine Place, Broad Marsh, under very distressing circumstances.

His landlady, Mrs. Stones, went as usual to Chapel and left the deceased apparently enjoying the best of health, on her return about 8 p.m., she found the door open and the aged veteran was lying on the hearth; help was immediately obtained, the doctor arrived very quickly but pronounced life extinct. The same medical man had attended the deceased for 20 years, and he said that no doubt the deceased was dead when he fell, the cause of death being heart failure.

W. Carlisle was born at Sutton, Notts., enlisted at Newcastle, August 28th, 1858, being then 25 years and 9 months old, was discharged 22nd July, 1865, after serving his country 7 years, 299 days, in her Majesty's army.

He was discharged "medically unfit" with a pension of tenpence per day, which was increased on the recommendation of the local Crimean and Indian Mutiny Veterans' Association to one shilling per day for life.

This gallant soldier fought with his regiment throughout the Crimean campaign and was awarded the Crimean and Turkish medals with clasp for Sebastopol.

The body will be interred in the veteran's ground in the General Cemetery on Thursday next at 1.30, with full military honours.

By kind permission of the Officers commanding, the Notts. Royal Horse Artillery will furnish gun carriage, while Non-commissioned Officers of the Robin Hood Rifles will act as bearers. The same regiment will provide firing and bugle parties.

The Rev. E. A. Simms will officiate at the interment.

Yours very faithfully,
p.p. Crimean and Indian Mutiny Veterans' Association,
H. SEELY WHITBY, *Joint Hon. Sec.*

100, ST. STEPHEN'S ROAD, SNEINTON, MAY 23RD, 1911.

Obituary Notice. Special notices were issued for veterans of the Crimean War. This notice was for W. Carlisle of Valentine Place, Broad Marsh. The Crimean War took place between 1854 and 1856 and was a bitter conflict fought on land and sea against Imperial Russia. The plight of many soldiers was underlined by the work of nurses like Florence Nightingale and Mary Seacole. Life could be very difficult for veterans, especially if they had suffered injuries, as a result of the war.

Nottinghamshire Archives M 1417

Sussex Street, Broad Marsh. The view is looking towards the Council House in 1931. The street was bustling with activity. Local residents in the area were served by a whole variety of shops and trades people along the length of the street.

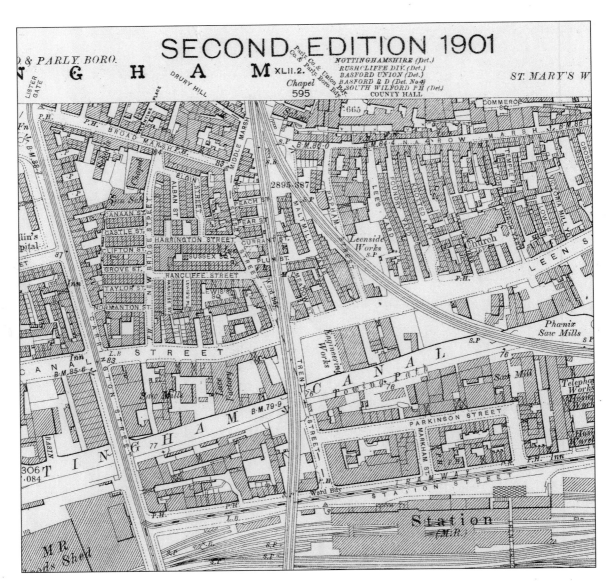

Ordnance Survey Map of 1901. It highlights the dense network of courtyards and alleys that once existed in Broad Marsh and Narrow Marsh.

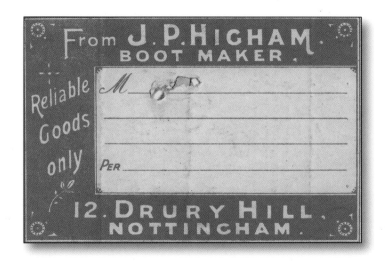

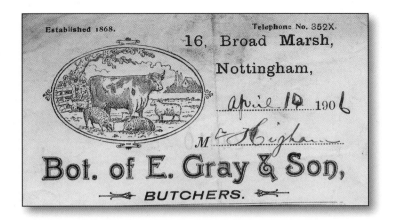

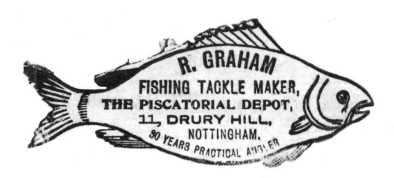

Invoices for Local Shops and Businesses. In Victorian and Edwardian times most everyday shopping was done at little stores within the local community. Butchers, grocers and bakers provided basic foodstuffs while shoes and boots would be repaired as often as possible. Fishing in the River and the Nottingham Canal was ever popular.

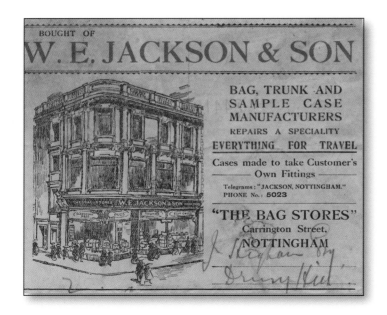

A 1915 Invoice for W.E. Jackson & Son.

The shop was described as 'The Bag Stores' of Carrington Street.

Jackson & Son of Carrington Street in 1959.

The building stood until redevelopment in the early 1970s. Jackson's was located in a prestigious building that attracted shoppers from all over Nottingham.

VALUABLE LEASEHOLD

SHOP and SHOWROOMS

Nos. 15 & 17, CARRINGTON STREET

(WITHIN A SHORT DISTANCE OF LISTER GATE)

With VACANT POSSESSION

To be offered for SALE BY AUCTION

on

Wednesday, 11th February, 1953

at 3 p.m.

Solicitors :
Messrs. BROWNE, JACOBSON & HALLAM,
44, Friar Lane,
Nottingham
(Tel. 44081).

Auctioneers :
Messrs. HENRY HALLAM & SON,
8, Low Pavement,
Nottingham
(Tel. 40091).

Estate Agent's Brochure. The brochure was for the sale of No's 15 & 17 Carrington Street, 1953. This main route, northwards, into the city centre from the Midland Station was blocked by the new Broad Marsh development of the 1970s. On the skyline there are typed markers for Woolworths, British Home Stores, Marks & Spencer and No's 15 & 17 Carrington Street.

Burton The Tailors.

The grand roof turret of Burton The Tailor's shop that once stood on the corner of Broad Marsh and Carrington Street. This photograph was taken in 1970. Burtons catered for a fashionable clientele.

Grey Friar Gate Car Park 1964.

This car park occupies a site at the junction of Greyfriar Street and Carrington Street. It was later covered by the shopping centre. The view is up Lister Gate towards the Council House.

Broad Marsh 1965. The view looks along Broad Marsh to Lister Gate. Dunn & Co., the tailors, is on the corner of the two streets and, on the same side of the street there is C&A, the fashion store, the Tower public house and a small newsagents.

Looking South From the Junction of Lister Gate and Carrington Street, 1964. The Sherwood Rooms, now the Ocean night club, Grey Friar Gate, can be seen on the right. Trolley bus cables are visible overhead.

Zebra Crossing. City Engineer's staff working at a zebra crossing in 1959. The shops on Carrington Street, in the background, were demolished a decade later.

View Looking Up Middle Pavement, 1968.

The large building on the corner was a Post Office. Severn's building is just visible on Middle Pavement.

View of Red Lion Street From Plumptre Square, c 1933. The building at the centre of the photograph is 'The Workman's Home'. The Town Arms is on the right of the photograph.

A View Looking Towards the City Centre. This view is from the Junction of Carrington Street and Canal Street, across the Broad Marsh bus station. This is a few years before the shopping centre was constructed when a temporary bus station was created to serve the south side of Nottingham.

Buses at Broad Marsh Bus Station. The bus station is seen here some years before the shopping centre was opened. The Centre incorporated a new, undercover bus station, to serve shoppers and commuters. High Pavement Chapel can just be seen at the top left.

Looking Northwards, Up Drury Hill Towards Middle Pavement, 1968.

The estate agents 'To Let' notice on one of the building underlines the street's decline as redevelopment loomed over the area.

The Entrance to Drury Hill, 1968.

The building on the right, that survived the redevelopment, was once the home of Abigail Gawthern, who wrote a detailed diary of her life and times between 1751 and 1810. It is now a café.

Looking Southwards Down Drury Hill, 1968.

It became part of the Broad Marsh Centre.

The Severn's Building 1969.

The building appears here in July 1969, not long before its removal to Castle Road. The building's mediaeval timbers have been exposed by demolition work on the adjoining building.

THE PROTESTERS

BY HARRY MARTIN

The voice of legitimate protest in a city which is almost notorious for its contentiousness, belongs not to the long-haired, left-wing intellectuals fired with the burning zeal of youth to put the world to rights, but a genteel group of little old ladies. And it is their frail shoulders which bear the burden of the battle to preserve Nottingham's historic heritage . . .

The Protestors, 1970.
A group of protestors led by Miss E.M. Palmer who campaigned to save the old streets and the cave system of Broad Marsh.

The Broad Marsh Centre Under Construction in 1973. The multi-storey car park has been completed.

New Escalator. A new escalator arrives at the Broad Marsh Centre, May 1974. Drury Hill was to become Drury Walk in the new Centre. A new era of shopping was arriving in Nottingham, with malls, escalators and a wide range of shops in a single building.

Construction Work In Progress. This photograph shows construction work in progress, in June 1973, on the Broad Marsh Shopping Centre. Shops on Lister Gate, including Woolworths, and The Sawyer's Arms, can be seen in the background.

Workmen, 1974.
These workmen are building a wall at the new Co-op store in the Broad Marsh Centre.

Broad Marsh Centre, Shortly After Opening in 1974. The future Co-op store is nearing completion. At that time there was a row of fountains in the concourse.

Official Opening. Photograph taken on 25 March 1975 at the official opening of the Broad Marsh Centre by the Duke of Gloucester.

The Collin Street Entrance to Broad Marsh, February 1974. Part of Carrington Street was demolished to make way for the Centre. The former road link to the city centre was cut-off to traffic.

Waterwheel. This large waterwheel once stood on the Lower Mall in the Shopping Centre.

Interior View of the Shopping Centre, 1975. This view of the Broad Marsh Centre shows one of the shops, Witney's, and a large, hollow, wooden caterpillar for children. This was later removed.

Soft Furnishings. The 'Soft Furnishings' Department of the Broad Marsh Co-op. The Co-op store opened on 31 October 1974.

Canteen Ladies of the Co-op Restaurant in 1974

Hosiery Counter of the Co-op in 1977. By this time the Centre was fully open. The site of the Co-op is now (2007) occupied by T- K Max.

Advert for Wimpy, 1974. The Centre had only just opened and the café had vacancies for both full-time staff and 'Saturday girls'.

Advert for the Fashion Store of Newman Granger, 1974.

Dennis McCarthy. Radio Nottingham personality Dennis McCarthy appears here in the late 1970s interviewing a shopper at the Co-op, Broad Marsh who had won a competition.

Broad Marsh Bus Station. Broad Marsh bus station provided covered-in accommodation for buses and modern facilities for shoppers and bus passengers.

Garner's Hill. A view at the top end of Garners Hill looking towards the east side of Broad Marsh in 2006. Steps down Garners Hill led down the side of Broad Marsh and gave access to a side entrance to the Centre.

An Interior View of Broad Marsh in 2007.

Acknowledgments

All the illustrations are published courtesy of Nottinghamshire Archives, except the following......

Sussex Street, Broad Marsh, photographs in 1928 and 1931 *(photographer F.W.Stevenson, permission Mrs M. Sentence) via Nottingham City Council Leisure and Community Services, Nottingham Central Library.*

Broad Marsh Bus Station (High Pavement Chapel in background) *private collection.*

View towards the City from Canal street; official opening of Broad Marsh Centre; interior views of Shopping centre with waterwheel and caterpillar; Broad Marsh Bus Station with bus; Artist's Impression *Westfield, Broad Marsh Centre.*

Broad Marsh Centre: escalator; construction in progress, 1973; workmen building wall; mall concourse after centre opening, 1974; Soft Furnishings Dep't ; Canteen Ladies; Hosiery Counter; Dennis McCarthy *The Co-operative Society.*

Cliff Road 2006; view at top of Garner's Hill 2006; southern approach to Broad Marsh Centre (back cover) *Chris Weir.*

Broad Marsh Plan 2006 'Experience Nottinghamshire'.

The authors would also like to thank Dorothy Ritchie of the Nottingham Central Library and Janine Bone, Manager of the Broad Marsh Centre (Westfield) for their help and advice.

**Artist's Impression (2006) of the Proposed
21st Century Broad Marsh Centre.**